BREAKING INTO ADVERTISING

BREAKING INTO ADVERTISING

Making Your Portfolio Work for You

Ken Musto

 Van Nostrand Reinhold
New York

Copyright © 1988 by Van Nostrand Reinhold

Library of Congress Catalog Card Number 88-10347

ISBN 0-442-26432-1

Printed in the United States of America

Designed by Monika Grejniec

Van Nostrand Reinhold
115 Fifth Avenue
New York, New York 10003

Van Nostrand Reinhold (International) Limited
11 New Fetter Lane
London, EC4P 4EE, England

Van Nostrand Reinhold
480 La Trobe Street
Melbourne, Victoria 3000, Australia

Macmillan of Canada
Division of Canada Publishing Corporation
164 Commander Boulevard
Agincourt, Ontario M1S 3C7, Canada

16 15 14 13 12 11 10 9 8 7 6 5 4 3 2 1

Library of Congress Cataloging in Publication Data
Musto, Ken
   Breaking into advertising: making your portfolio work for you/
Ken Musto.
      p.   cm.
   ISBN 0-442-26432-1 (pbk.)
   1. Advertising.   2. Job hunting.   I. Title.
HF5827.M88   1988
659.1′023′73—dc19   88-10347
                                                  CIP

CONTENTS

FOREWORD

If I could, I'd pass a law. It would ban all would-be copywriters and art directors from looking for a job until they have read this book.

Breaking In should be the bible for any aspiring copywriter or art director. The tips, techniques, and insights presented are invaluable. This book will do for beginners what the paddle did for canoeing.

As head of one of New York's largest creative placement agencies, I see many people trying to get into this business. Most of them have no idea what agencies are looking for in a portfolio. It's sad to see what people are hitting the streets with: portfolios that are amateurish-looking, that lack focus and substance.

Unfortunately, I have to tell many of them to go back to school and learn how to do it right. Now I can tell them to read *Breaking In!* Ken Musto tells it like it is. There's no fat in this book, no wasted words—just good clear advice. When you're done reading, you'll know exactly what you have to do to make your portfolio look like a professional's.

Not only do you get all the secrets for putting a great portfolio together, you get something else beginners don't know much about—how to look for a job in advertising.

My advice to anyone starting out: Read this book and re-read it. Don't put it down until you've memorized it. Do this, and you'll have a much better chance of breaking in.

Dale Cunningham
President
The Dale Cunningham Creative Placement Agency

ACKNOWLEDGMENTS

To Monika Grejniec, who designed the book.

To Richard Wilde, of the School of Visual Arts, who encouraged me to put all this down in a book.

To my editor, Cindy Zigmund, who showed me how to make things better.

To my friends Ray Dempsey, Jean Lehman, Frank DeVito, Bob Steigleman, John Triolo, Marilyn Pocius, Phil Balshi, and Ira Chynsky for their insightful contributions.

To my former students, Karen Gallo, Beth Griffen, Peter Favat and Ken Musto, Jr. for letting me use their excellent work.

To Frank Tedesco for his time and patience in photographing all this work.

To Dave Content for his terrific illustrations.

And finally, to Mary Musto, the best critic a writer could ever want.

INTRODUCTION

How do you get that first job as a copywriter or art director? It's simple. You have to show how good you are. To do that, you have to put together a terrific portfolio of sample ads.

This book will tell you, in simple, easy-to-understand language, just how to do that. If you follow the guidelines, your chances of getting the all-important first job will be much easier.

First of all, whether your goal is to be an art director or a copywriter, keep one thing in mind: your portfolio should contain only ads.

Future art directors should not include mechanicals they did of the high school prom program or sketches from a still-life class. These may show that you have talent, but they don't show that you know how to put together an ad.

Future copywriters should not include articles from their college newspaper, short stories, or school plays. Those pieces may show that you can write, but they don't show that you can write advertising copy.

Advertising is the business of selling products. Every ad is an opportunity to promote a relationship with a customer. When you're writing an ad, you are, in fact, selling, even if money isn't changing hands. What people hiring you want to see is how well you sell a product.

There is no magic formula for creating great advertisements, but there is a formula for putting a portfolio together—a portfolio that will make people sit up and take notice of your work, a portfolio that will get you a job.

I

THE PORTFOLIO

Always remember that your portfolio is a reflection of you. How you think. How you work. You should always resist the usual. Be bright. Be imaginative. There is nothing worse than a dull ad in your portfolio.

Equally important is how the portfolio looks. A clean, crisp, orderly portfolio is much easier for someone to look at than a messy one. So keep in mind that neatness counts. A good portfolio should consist of fifteen ads. You can include two or three more if you want, but fifteen is the minimum. People at advertising agencies are usually busy, and they want to go through a portfolio quickly. I have found a potential employer can look at fifteen ads in a minimum amount of time and still judge how good you are.

You should break the fifteen down as follows. Include three campaigns made up of three ads each for a total of nine pieces. (A campaign is a series of ads with a single goal or a single advertising objective.) Campaigns are very important in your portfolio. Most people can create a single ad on one product. Campaigns show how you would sustain an idea over time, which is important. If you don't have campaigns in your portfolio it will show an obvious weakness. The balance of your portfolio should be made up of six ads on individual products.

Should you decide to do more than three campaigns, that's great. You'll make your portfolio even better. Four campaigns look stronger than three, and five campaigns look even stronger than four. The more the better. But end up with fifteen pieces in total.

The type of ads you choose to work on is important. Don't do all public service ads. Child abuse and drug addiction are emotional and shocking subjects. But they are relatively easy to do advertising for, as compared with selling a product.

Stick with packaged goods. Packaged goods are products sold mostly in supermarkets or drugstores such as deodorants, toothpastes, dog foods, coffees, mouthwashes, and the like.

Work on some ads that offer a service: airlines, car rentals, a hotel, etc. Create ads about a country. Or if you prefer, invent a product and make up ads for it. Pick products that seem difficult to sell, and show how you would sell them.

Go through a magazine, pick out what you think are bad ads, and show how you'd make them better.

Don't work on products that are associated with successful campaigns. Stay away, for example, from products like Volkswagen, Chivas Regal, and BMW. They are classics, and at this stage in your career you won't be able to beat them.

Prepare Print Ads Only

Don't bother to put television commercials in your portfolio. First, these are harder to do well than print ads, and second, very few people bother to read television commercials in a portfolio. They are cumbersome to get through and usually have to be explained when shown. Most of the time you won't be present when someone is looking at your work.

Third, you really don't need television commercials to get an entry-level job. I've never seen or heard of a beginner being turned down for a job because of a lack of television commercials in a portfolio. People looking to hire beginners don't expect them to know how to put together television commercials.

Most agencies bring "juniors" along slowly. Assistant art directors, for instance, do just what their title implies: assist art directors. So, whether you're hired as a junior writer or a junior art director, you'll cut your teeth on assignments like small space ads, trade ads, or collateral pieces. It will be quite some time before you're trusted with a television assignment.

Stick to print ads for one very good reason: it's much easier for you to get your ideas down as print ads. What's more, your idea will look far more powerful in a print ad than buried somewhere in a television commercial. Most great advertising is best remembered in print.

However, if you insist on trying television commercials, read through chapter 7 carefully.

The same goes for radio commercials. Forget them. People don't read them.

Fifteen bright, creative, strategically sound print ads are all you need to knock someone's socks off and land a good job.

2

PUTTING TOGETHER AN ART DIRECTOR'S PORTFOLIO

In addition to great ideas, a polished look to an art director's portfolio is extremely important. It pays for an aspiring art director to prepare tight layouts with magic markers. It shows how well you can put together a layout. (If you can't draw, take a course.)

Design each ad so that it has its own personality. Your ads should not look all alike, with the same basic layout and the same type face. That shows you're in a rut.

Individuality is especially important in ad campaigns. Give each one an identity. Make them look like campaigns. It's hard work, but it's worth it. What's more, it's good discipline. As an art director, creating campaigns is something you'll be required to do during your entire advertising career.

Prepare your ads in color, unless of course, you've intentionally designed something to be in black-and-white.

If you prefer, use transfer type or instant lettering for your headlines, but doing them by hand is better. It shows another skill.

Forget photography. Illustrate your visuals. Keep in mind that you're looking for a job as an art director, not as a photographer.

Forget body copy. You don't need it. That's for future copywriters.

Concentrate on ideas, headlines, layouts, and design.

Mount all your ads on styrofoam. Make them all the same size. Wrap them in a lightweight acetate for protection. Put all your ads in a hard case about 17″ × 22″ (fig. 2-1). You can get one at any art-supply store. It costs more than a zippered case but makes for a neater, more professional presentation of your work and will last a long time.

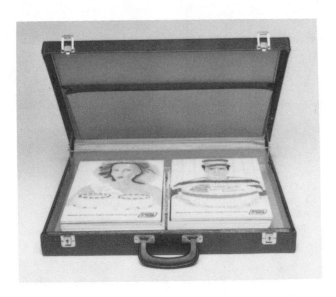

2-1. Hard cases cost a bit more, but make for a more professional presentation.

2-2. (above)   How to spray-mount your ads.

1. Spray the back of your layout with spray mount and let it dry completely.
2. Mount your ad on styrofoam board.
3. Burnish out all the bubbles.
4. With a razor blade, trim to the size you want.

2-3. (right)   How to dry-mount your ads.

Dry-mounting is a more permanent way of putting your ads down. If you have access to a hot-press machine I recommend dry-mounting instead of spray-mounting. Your ads will stay down for years.

1. Tack dry-mounting tissue to the back of your layout using a hot tacking iron.
2. Trim off the excess dry-mounting tissue so that it's flush with the edges of your layout.
3. Tack your ad to styrofoam board at all four corners.
4. Put your ad into the hot-press machine for 30 to 60 seconds at 200 to 250° F.
5. Trim to the desired size and your ad is mounted permanently.

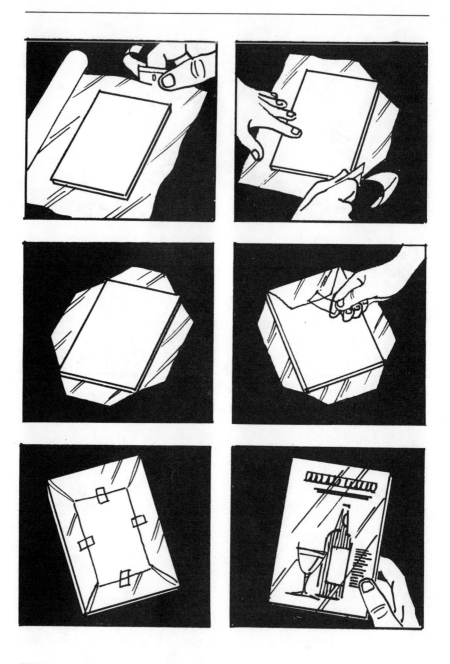

Take a look at two former students's portfolios, pictured in the color pages of this book. Note how tight the layouts are and how crisp and neat the ads are. Study the campaigns and their different looks.

With these portfolios, both students got good jobs with top New York advertising agencies. (Note that you don't see any television commercials here—only print ads.)

2-4. How to wrap your ads in acetate.
1. Start with number .0015 acetate. (It comes on a roll and is available in art-supply stores.) Place your mounted ad face down and cut out about three inches around all four sides.
2. Cut at right angles at all four corners.
3. Remove all excess acetate. This is what you should be left with.
4. Fold top flap over, pull tightly, and tape down.
5. Fold the bottom flap over, pull tightly, and tape. Then do the sides the same way.
Your ad will be well protected against smudges and fingerprints and will look presentable for years to come.

3

PUTTING TOGETHER A COPYWRITER'S PORTFOLIO

Like the art director's portfolio, the copywriter's book must be concerned with the same thing: ideas. But the portfolio does not need to look as polished. A copywriter's ads do not have to be tight, magic-marker layouts in color. They can be rough layouts, done by yourself, in black-and-white.

However, ads usually look terrible when copywriters try to lay them out. So if you want your portfolio to look more professional, get an art-director friend to lay your ads out for you. (I paid an art director to do my layouts and it was a terrific investment.)

But remember, if you do that, the ads have to be yours. You want your portfolio to be a reflection of you, not of someone else. So just give the art director your rough pencil sketches of what you think the ad should look like and let him copy them in a professional-looking way. Again, black-and-white is fine. If you feel you want to add a little color, do so, but it isn't necessary.

After you have the layout, prepare the body copy. Nobody gets a job as a copywriter without presenting body copy.

Creating good body copy is hard work. It requires writing and rewriting. It isn't easy. Work at it. Develop a style. Make it sing. It's a big part of what people look for in a copywriter, so don't take it lightly. For more on writing good body copy, see chapter 6.

All your ads should go into a zippered portfolio case about 14" x 17", with acetate-covered pages (fig. 3-1). You can get them at an art-supply store. Slip your ads under the acetate sheet on the right side; your body copy goes on the left side.

Your copy must be neatly typed. If you can't type, get someone to do it for you. I suggest that if you don't type, take a course. It's not a necessity for being a good

3-1. A zippered portfolio case showcases your body copy on one side and your ad layouts on the other.

writer, but it makes things a whole lot easier. For more detailed information on presenting your copy, see the following section.

Study the portfolios by two former copywriting students in figures 3-2 to 3-17. The layouts were done by art directors, but all the ideas were the students's.

Analyze the campaigns. Again, notice that there are no television commercials here.

Both students got jobs at major advertising agencies almost immediately after graduation.

Sample Ads from a Beginning Copywriter's Portfolio

3-2. Three-ad campaign.

3-3. Three-ad campaign.

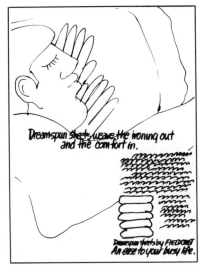

3-4. Three-ad campaign.

3-5, 3-6. Single ads.

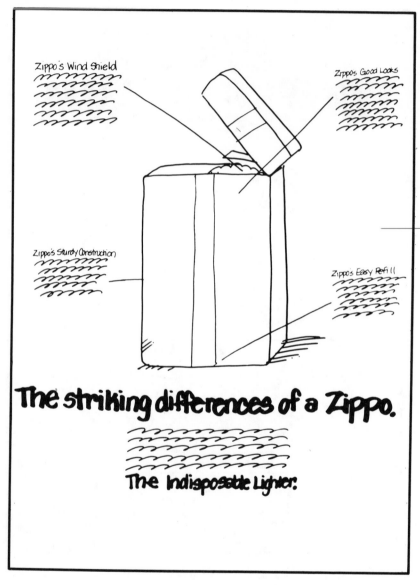

The striking differences of a Zippo.

The Indisposable Lighter.

3-7, 3-8. Single ads.

3-9, 3-10. Single ads.

We've got a polish that repairs the tops of kids' shoes.

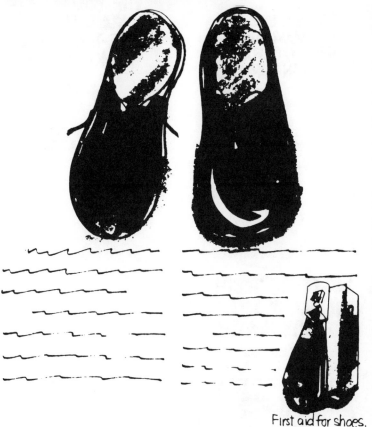

First aid for shoes.

More of What a Beginning Copywriter's Portfolio Should Look Like

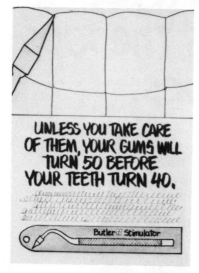

UNLESS YOU TAKE CARE OF THEM, YOUR GUMS WILL TURN 50 BEFORE YOUR TEETH TURN 40.

Butler Stimulator

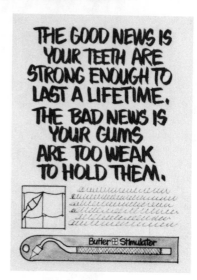

THE GOOD NEWS IS YOUR TEETH ARE STRONG ENOUGH TO LAST A LIFETIME. THE BAD NEWS IS YOUR GUMS ARE TOO WEAK TO HOLD THEM.

Butler Stimulator

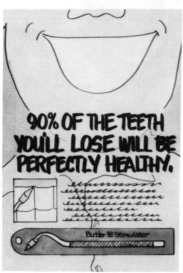

90% OF THE TEETH YOU'LL LOSE WILL BE PERFECTLY HEALTHY.

Butler Stimulator

3-11. Three-ad campaign.

3-12. Three-ad campaign.

3-13. Three-ad campaign.

IF YOU CAN'T AFFORD TO MOVE, GET A BED THAT DOES.

WE MAKE BEDS THAT MAKE ROOM.

MURPHY BEDS. WE MAKE BEDS THAT MAKE ROOM.

HOW TO GO FROM A LIVING ROOM TO A DINING ROOM TO A BEDROOM WITHOUT LEAVING THE ROOM.

MURPHY BEDS. WE MAKE BEDS THAT MAKE ROOM.

3-14. Three-ad campaign.

3-15, 3-16. Single ads.

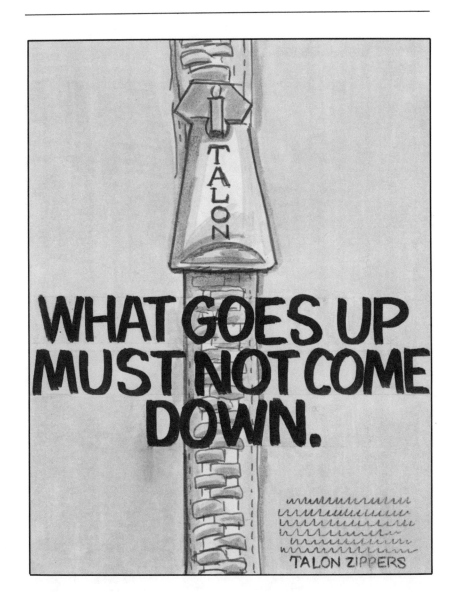

3-17. Single ad.

4

PRESENT YOUR COPY LIKE A PRO

There are basic dos and don'ts in copywriting that, surprisingly, are often ignored:

- Lay out your body copy so that it *looks* inviting to read.
- Put headlines in all caps and center them over the body copy.
- Put body copy in upper- and lowercase letters, never all caps.
- Single-space the body copy using narrow measures, which make for easier reading than wide measures.
- Leave at least an inch and a half margin on both sides of the body copy.
- Use short paragraphs. They're easier to read than big blocks of type.
- Indent when you start a new paragraph.
- End up with your product name in all caps and your tag line, if you have one, in upper- and lowercase, directly under it.

Take a look at the sample in figure 4.1 and use it as your guide. Remember, be neat and *no typos please*.

HEALS CUTS, SCRAPES AND SCRATCHES.

        Nobody beats up a pair of shoes and knocks
them out of commission faster than a kid.
        Which is why we have first aid for shoes.
        Esquire Scuffcote.
        It helps shoes survive kids.
        Not only does Scuffcote get shoes back
on their feet with a great shine, but it also fills
in cuts and scrapes, heals scratches, and covers
up minor irritations of the leather.
        So now when a pair of battered and bruised
shoes come home after a hard day at the play-
ground, you know how to heal their wounds.

        ESQUIRE SCUFFCOTE
        First aid for shoes.

4-1. Sample of typed body copy.

5

PREPARE A WORK PLAN BEFORE YOU START

Most beginning writers and art directors make the mistake of trying to create ads without focus and direction. The result is that they don't know where to begin. They grope, they flounder, and they end up doing ads that are off-base and not well thought-out.

A work plan is extremely important. It's your creative strategy, your blueprint for building an ad or a campaign. It's your road map for getting from a blank sheet of paper to a finished ad.

The job of a copywriter or an art director isn't just to create advertising. It's to create ads that *sell*. One thing that helps to make that happen is finding a usable strategy and sticking with it.

Before you can dig for ideas that are strong and meaningful, you need to have discipline. The work plan gives you that discipline.

I look at the work plan as serving another useful purpose. Creative people seem to be right-brained thinkers—intuitive, abstract, artistic. And those are great assets. Creative individuals want to get into advertising because they feel the need to talk and reach out to people. But being only a right-brained person makes for only half an ad maker. The work plan forces creatives to think like left-brained folks—in a way that's businesslike, practical, logical. The people in our business who combine those two ways of thinking are the ones making the best, most effective advertising.

Without a work plan to guide them, even the most experienced writers and art directors would be lost. You shouldn't begin any work without one.

Let's say you decide to do an ad campaign on a foreign country. Research it first. Find out as much as you can about that country. Go to the library. Go to travel agents and pick up brochures. Absorb all you can. Then sit down and make your work plan.

You'll find that the work plan will give you greater knowledge of your product, which in turn will help you to put together better ads.

Here's a simple way to write up a work plan. In addition, take a look at the sample plans on pages 43 and 44.

A work plan should consist of the following points:

The Objective. This is what you want the ad to do.
The Prospect. This is the person you are talking to in the ad.
The Benefit. This is what the person reading your ad will get if he or she buys the product.
The Reasons Why. These are support for the benefit.

With your work plan done, begin to write your ad. As the ad takes shape, look at the work plan to make sure that you are following your strategy.

Be careful though. Don't fall into the trap of making your ad sound exactly like the work plan. The work plan is for direction, not for creativity. Your ad must be bright, imaginative, inventive, and on target.

Every advertising agency uses a work plan in some shape or form, so it's a good idea to get used to working with them now. It'll make doing your ads easier, and it'll help keep you on the right track.

SAMPLE WORK PLAN

PRODUCT: Honey

OBJECTIVE: Give prospects a reason to use honey.

PROSPECT: People who use sugar and sugar substitutes.

BENEFIT: Honey is a delicious, wholesome way to sweeten many of your favorite foods.

REASONS WHY: Honey is all natural.
Honey is as sweet as sugar.
Honey has nutritional value.
It contains some vitamins and minerals.
Honey can be used virtually everywhere sugar or a sugar substitute is used: in coffee, tea, cereal, baking, cooking, etc.
Sugar and sugar substitutes have no food value.

SAMPLE WORK PLAN

PRODUCT: Computer dating service

OBJECTIVE: Give prospects a reason to use a com-
                    puter dating service.

PROSPECT: Men and women, age 24 and over.

BENEFIT: A computer dating service is a sensi-
                    ble, fun way to meet a mate.

REASONS WHY: Each applicant is thoroughly inter-
                    viewed.
                    You're given a printout and photos of
                    prospective dates beforehand.
                    Computer scientifically matches your
                    likes and dislikes with others.
                    You only meet the people you choose
                    to meet.
                    Computer dating lets you avoid the
                    hassles of singles bars, resorts, and
                    classified ads.

6

HOW TO PUT TOGETHER A GOOD AD

I don't have much use for rules. They only rule out the possibility of doing terrific work. What's more, if you try to perfect a formula for doing ads, you won't be doing good ones for long.

Advertising is emotional and intellectual. It should be done with your head and your instincts, and you need to find the right balance between the two. In short, a good idea comes from two things: tough, analytical thinking about the marketplace, plus imagination.

I can't tell you how to make great ads specifically, but I can give you guidelines, tips, and some general direction. First, after you've picked the product you want to work on, learn all about it. Feel it. Taste it. Wear it. Get to know its strongest selling point. Make sure you have all the facts you can gather. Without them, you won't be able to be logical or persuasive.

Next, take the time to map out a work plan, a strategy, for yourself. Make it as precise as you can. Believe it or not, a precise work plan will allow you more creative freedom than a vague one will. If that sounds like a contradiction, it's not. A loose work plan will restrict you because you won't know where to go with it. A precise one will open your mind.

After you've completed your work plan, and it makes sense to you, then and only then should you begin to put down some ideas and write some head-lines. Remember your objectives, what you've set out to do. Remember to give your prospect a benefit in your ad, a reason to buy your product.

Remember that an ad must have a concept, and that concept should come out of the product. Try to make your ads fresh and *original*. (Creating advertising *means* creating, not imitating.) But don't ever try to be so fresh and original that your point is missed and your ad becomes silly and dumb. A billiant creative irrelevant ad, just like a dull ad, will never sell a product—or convince someone to hire you.

One thing worth mentioning at this point: There is no *one* solution to an ad. There are many. But the ad you're working on is always an answer to someone's business problem.

Get your message across in the headline. We know for a fact that most people don't read past the headline. If you rely on your body copy to tell the story you've wasted your time. Write dozens of headlines. Write your headlines and your body copy the way people talk.

Work on developing a style. Read different ads and you'll see what I mean by style. The good ads have it, the dull ones don't. Ads that are written with a style present all the facts about the product in an interesting, enjoyable way.

Don't try to show off when you write. Don't try to be clever. Don't substitute a cute technique for good thinking. People see right through it. You're better off just taking your reader through your argument, step by step.

Long headlines and long body copy are nothing to be afraid of. If they work, use them.

Don't be lazy. Write and rewrite the body copy until it sparkles. No matter how hard you've worked on it, you can always make it better. I've never written a piece of body copy less than six times. And every time I rewrite, the copy gets tighter, punchier, and easier to read.

Monosyllables work best. Say what you want to say simply. Don't beat around the bush. Most great advertising is simple. That's how people talk, and that's the style that is most appealing to read. Keep in mind that people don't have time to figure out what you're trying to say.

If you come up with an idea, and you're not sure if it's good, let it age for a while. Go back to it in a day or two. If it still feels good, chances are you've got it. If it doesn't, start over.

Look at your ad and ask yourself: Does it follow your strategy? Is it interesting? Is it informative? Is it honest? Is it emotional? Is it unusual? If your ad passes these tests, put it in your book.

7

HOW TO PREPARE A TELEVISION COMMERCIAL

By now you know how I feel about television commercials in a beginner's portfolio—they're a waste of
time and effort. I see a lot of portfolios and I hardly
ever bother reading storyboards. Like most people in
this business I'm usually very busy. I want to go through
a portfolio quickly, and television commercials are hard
to read and complicated. I remember how hard I
worked on them for my own portfolio and how they
were virtually ignored.

Spend your time creating the kinds of ads that will
get noticed: good, solid print pieces. If, in spite of all this,
you still want to do a few commercials for your portfolio, here are some tips.

Don't just put scripts in your portfolio. Lay out
your commercials on television storyboards. A storyboard is just what the name implies: a board that tells a
story. Your commercial should tell a story in 30 or 60
seconds, depending on the length of the ad.

First, get yourself a storyboard pad. They're like
layout pads, are available at most art-supply stores, and
are relatively inexpensive (fig. 7-1).

7-1. Use a storyboard to present a television commercial.

Draw your visuals in each frame. Position your copy below, or next, to each frame, depending on your type of storyboard (fig. 7-2).

A 30-second commercial uses eight frames and about 65 words. A 60-second spot, 16 frames and about 130 words. Spell out your video instructions below each frame, i.e., camera moves, dissolves, cuts, and so on.

7-2. Draw your visuals in each frame, with the copy below or to the side.

The easiest way to do a commercial is to think of it as a comic strip telling a short story. Keep it simple. Concentrate on the idea. Don't let your idea get lost in the storyboard. And don't try to impress people with a lot of technical television terms. Remember, you're a beginner and not required to know all those things. Ideas are what will get you a job.

8

HOW TO LOOK FOR A JOB IN ADVERTISING

For beginning copywriters and art directors, the hardest job in advertising is getting that first job. In almost all other fields, company recruiters invade colleges and universities each year, looking for and snatching up graduates. There is no such luxury for creative people wanting to get into advertising. Advertising personnel don't come looking for *you*. You have to go out and find *them*. Later on in your career, as you get better and more experienced, all that will change. But unfortunately, that's how it is in the beginning.

Understandably, the question most often asked—and worried over—is "How and where do I begin to look for a job?" Here are some tips to start you off in the right direction.

First, make a list of all the commercials and ads that you like and think are good. Next, find out which agencies are doing those ads and go after them. Here's how.

Get hold of a book called the *Standard Directory of Advertising Agencies*, otherwise known as The Agency Red Book. It's available from the public library, and any college or university with courses in advertising should have it in their library.

The Agency Red Book lists all the advertising agencies worldwide. It gives you the cities they are in,

8-1. Two of the best-kept secrets in the business.

including their branch offices and where they're located. It tells you the size of the agency and it lists all the accounts it handles.

The most important information this book gives you is the names and titles of the key people in the Creative Department—the people you want and need to reach. It also lists telephone numbers and addresses, so you've got everything to get you started right under your nose. What's more, The Agency Red Book comes out three times a year, so you know the information is reasonably accurate and up-to-date.

If you can't get your hands on an Agency Red Book, call any advertising agency in your area. The good-sized ones all have their own libraries. Simply tell them you're a student and you'd like to use their Agency Red Book for reference. Most will be glad to have you come over and will help you out. Don't be bashful. Call.

If for whatever reason that doesn't work, get in touch with the publishers of the Agency Red Book at National Register Publishing Company, 3004 Glenview Road, Wilmette, IL 60091.

Another good source for reaching agencies is the Creative Black Book. This book lists all the agencies, along with addresses and telephone numbers, in the United States and Canada. It doesn't, unfortunately, give you the names of people to contact, size of the agency, or accounts it handles. It does, however, list the names, addresses, and telephone numbers of employment agencies around the country who place creative people.

While it's not as comprehensive as the Agency Red Book, the Creative Black Book is an excellent alternative. Agency libraries will have this resource.

If you can't find a copy, contact the publishers of the Creative Black Book directly at 401 Park Avenue South, New York, NY 10016.

Armed with agencies, names of people and telephone numbers, you've now got a good start.

The Profile of a Creative Department

Before you go knocking on doors, you need to understand the makeup of the Creative Department of an ad agency. The majority are structured along the same basic lines, especially at the big agencies. Figure 8-2 shows the typical breakdown.

The department is headed by the Creative Director. Under the Creative Director are the Group Creative Directors or Associate Creative Directors. The title depends on the agency and its size. (Some agencies even toss in another level called Creative Supervisor as part of their structure.)

Next come the teams of copywriters and art directors. The last level—your level right now—is made up of assistant art directors and beginning copywriters. The number of people in each of these levels is determined by the size of the agency.

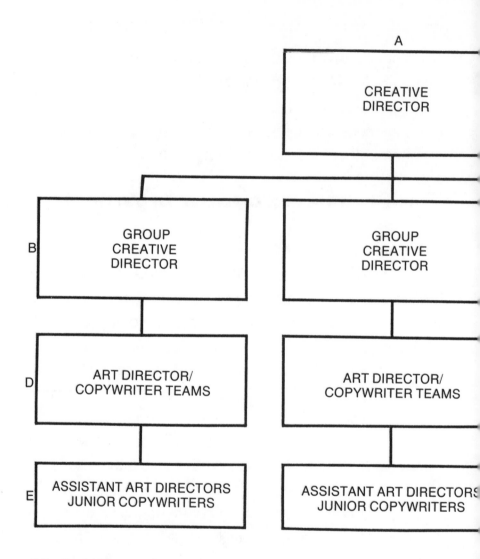

A

CREATIVE
DIRECTOR

B

GROUP
CREATIVE
DIRECTOR

GROUP
CREATIVE
DIRECTOR

D

ART DIRECTOR/
COPYWRITER TEAMS

ART DIRECTOR/
COPYWRITER TEAMS

E

ASSISTANT ART DIRECTORS
JUNIOR COPYWRITERS

ASSISTANT ART DIRECTORS
JUNIOR COPYWRITERS

8-2. Creative Department flow chart.

A. Creative Director—head of the department.

B. Executive Creative Director, Group Creative Director, or Associate Creative Director, depending on the agency and its size.

C. Creative Department Recruiter or "headhunter." The big agencies have them, the smaller shops do not.

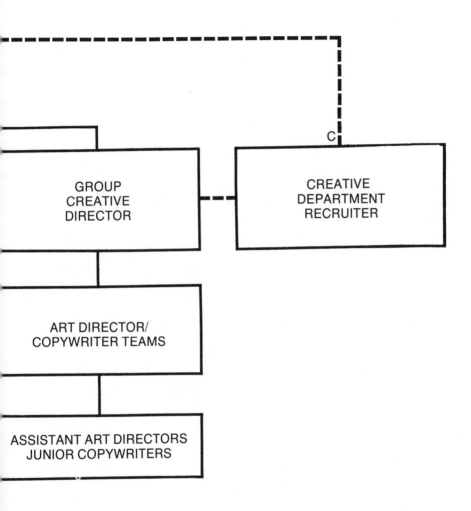

C

GROUP CREATIVE DIRECTOR

CREATIVE DEPARTMENT RECRUITER

ART DIRECTOR/ COPYWRITER TEAMS

ASSISTANT ART DIRECTORS JUNIOR COPYWRITERS

D. Copywriter/art director teams. How many teams are in each group depends on the size of the agency.

E. Assistant art directors and beginning (junior) copywriters. Again, the number of people working in each group depends on the agency size. Here is where you'll be trying to break in at the beginning.

A key player in the Creative Department is the Creative Recruiter. This is a position you'll find in most big agencies today, because many Creative Departments do their own hiring. The Personnel Department hires for the rest of the agency. It's the Creative Recruiter's responsibility to call in portfolios to help fill openings and to look for talented people for future jobs.

While the recruiter is not the final word on hiring, this is one person you should try to get in touch with. However, anyone on the flowchart in figure 8.2 could be important to you. You never know who might take a liking to your work and recommend you. I've seen agencies that have no job openings take a liking to a portfolio and hire the person right on the spot.

Call, Don't Write

Résumés and letters tend to be filed and forgotten. Besides, résumés and letters will never be able to show how talented you are. So call, find out who at a particular agency looks at portfolios, and ask to drop your work off.

Find out which ad agencies have internships or training programs. Such programs are the exception rather than the rule, but if you can find one and get into it, it's a fantastic opportunity. But the only way you'll find out is by calling and asking.

Look into the employment agencies that specialize in placing people in advertising. Some charge a fee when they place you, but most of them have jobs that are fee-paid. There are a number of these agencies in New York, Los Angeles, Chicago, Dallas, and Atlanta.

Try corporations and department stores. Most have their own advertising departments. Many good writers and art directors have come up that way.

Try the television networks. They also do a lot of in-house advertising and are always on the lookout for talent.

Try every route you can think of. If you have friends in the business, ask them if they know of any jobs or other people you can see or call. Again, don't be bashful.

Don't Give Up

If you've been rejected by an agency once, don't count yourself out for good. For instance, if someone in the Creative Department turns you down, find out the names of other people in that same department and start all over. In most agencies, especially the big ones, one person usually doesn't know all the hiring needs of a company.

It's helpful to keep a list of the people you've sent your book to. Note the dates you saw a given person and what was said about your work.

Should you show your portfolio to people in personnel departments? My advice is to avoid it like the plague. Most of them wouldn't recognize a good portfolio. The people you want to see are all in the Creative Department.

Two Portfolios Are Better than One

If you have the time and the patience, make up a second portfolio. It'll give you twice the chance for getting your work around. I never quite understood why more writers and art directors don't do this. Be sure that the duplicate portfolio is just as crisp and neat as the original. In fact, they should both be originals.

It's unavoidable in the advertising business that portfolios can get tied up at an agency for a while, but don't get impatient. Give people a week or so to hold onto your portfolio. After that, it's okay to call and ask if it's been looked at, and if you can have it back. But only ask for it back if you really need it.

If someone wants to look at your portfolio while it's at another agency, call and politely explain the situation and tell them you'll get the portfolio back in a few days. That happens often in the business, and it's quite acceptable.

It Only Takes One Yes

Through all of this you'll be getting a lot of rejections. Try as hard as you can to remain thick-skinned.

Most of the time rejections are not based on the work in a portfolio. Salary considerations, level of experience, chemistry between people, or just plain lack of openings have much to do with why you don't land a job.

Hang in there. And don't be timid. I admire the people who can cut through all the "layers," get to someone's office, drop a portfolio on the desk and force them to take a look. Remember, all you need is one yes.

Sample Ads from a Beginning Art Director's Portfolio

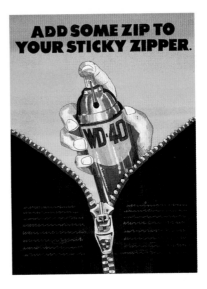

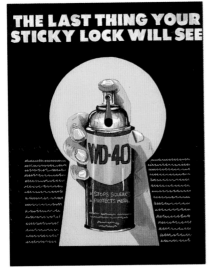

Three-ad campaign.

Three-ad campaign.

Three-ad campaign.

Single ad.

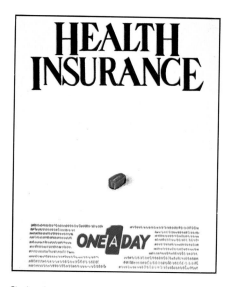

Single ad.

Single ad.

Single ad.

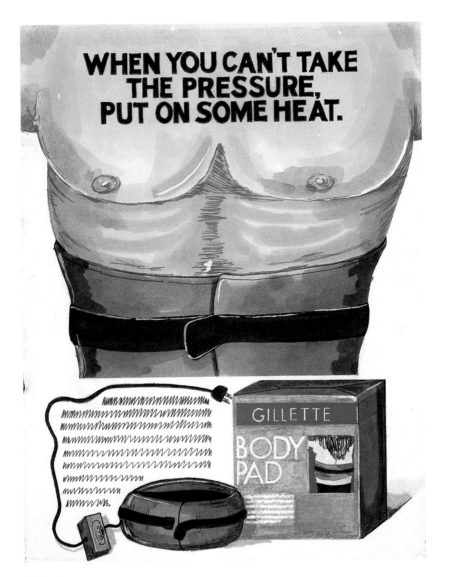

Single ad.

Single ad.

Another Sample of a Beginning Art Director's Portfolio

Three-ad campaign.

What good is a dishwashing detergent if it doesn't remove elbow grease?

The straight-to-the-dishwasher detergent

Is this the first wash cycle your dishes go through?

The straight-to-the-dishwasher detergent

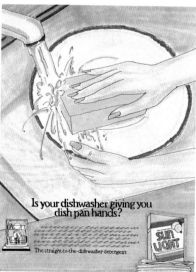

Is your dishwasher giving you dish pan hands?

The straight-to-the-dishwasher detergent

Three-ad campaign.

Three-ad campaign.

Some pedigrees should be seen and not heard.

adopt a mutt

Single ad.

A portion that keeps you in proportion.

Single ad.

Single ad.

surprise her with some precious minerals.

Single ad.

Single ad.

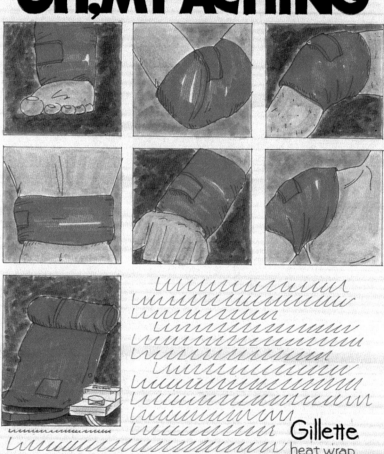

Single ad.

9

WHAT THE PROS LOOK FOR

I want you to meet some people who work at advertising agencies who look at portfolios. They range from President/Creative Directors to a Creative Supervisor to a Creative Department Recruiter. They are copywriters or art directors by trade and are typical of the people who will ultimately have the say on whether or not you get a job. They are tough and demanding and they know what they want. I wanted to give them a chance to speak so you don't get any surprises when you begin looking for a job.

9-1. Frank DeVito. President, Creative Director.

'I look for strong art direction and visual ideas.'

First and foremost, what I look for in a beginning art director's book is *ideas*. I want to see how a creative person thinks.

I look for freshness and audacity. A portfolio is prepared without a client, and that is a distinct advantage. There are no rules. There are no don'ts. A beginner's book should be free of these shackles. So I look for a book that takes chances. If they don't take chances without a client, when will they?

Next, I look for strong art direction and visual

ideas. Most books I see have strong headlines, and the art direction seems secondary. What I'm hiring is an *art director*. I want to see how a person thinks visually. Does the visual give an added dimension to the idea? Can the visual stand on its own? Does the visual make the headline work harder?

I also look for freshness of layout. All too often, what I see is a standard layout. No thinking has gone into making the layout itself special.

I then look at the craft. How does the book look? Is it neat and professionally put together? Does the person show a good knowledge of type? Can he or she put ideas down on paper?

Campaigns are helpful. Is the idea more than a one-shot?

A portfolio is a sales tool. Not only does it show you know how to sell products, it also sells yourself. And that's the point. Do anything that will help to sell *you*. Make your portfolio distinctive, so it stands out from the many that it will be competing with.

The next step is the interview. It should be taken very seriously. Sell your good points. Will a prospective employer want you to work for him or her? Remember, you'll be spending many hours together. Chemistry is important, so try to make a good impression.

9-2. Marilyn Pocius. Vice President. Associate Creative Director.

'The easiest way to convince me that you're an idea person is to show me a series of ads.'

What I want to see in a beginning copywriter's portfolio is concepts. I need to see that you can find and express a selling idea in words and pictures that are simple and compelling. Simple is the hard part. If your idea is sound, it should come through loud and clear in a print ad.

So what's a concept? It could be as elegant as all those Volkswagen ads or as schlocky as "consumes 47 times its weight in stomach acid." Having a concept doesn't necessarily make a good ad, but it's a start. A concept can be words or pictures, but it's almost always the two working together. If the headline and the visual are communicating the same thing, you're being redundant.

The easiest way to convince me that you're an idea person is to show me a series of ads. A really good concept has "legs"—it can run for a long time. It'll work in many different ways. A really good concept is one I want to improve, play off of. Headlines and visuals pop to mind. So take it as a compliment.

I don't care if there's television in your portfolio. I do like to see body copy so I know you can write more than five or ten words without freaking out. There are no rules about the number of pieces, but looking at more than twenty would make me unhappy. Learn to edit. I often see every thought a writer has ever had in his or her portfolio. Everybody loves all their own ideas, at least when they're newborn. Put away your portfolio for a few days and take a surprise look at it. Read headlines out loud to your bathroom mirror. Explain an ad to a friend. Still love it?

You should be prepared for conflicting criticism of your work. The ad I think is brilliant will have the next guy telling you to take it out of your book. What you personally think is good counts. That's your style. Edit to please yourself, or you'll end up schizophrenic.

It's okay to scare me. In fact, it's a sure way to make me remember you. There'll be time enough for safe ads when real clients demand them. Surprise me with the unusual. Invent a marketing concept or a product: pet rocks? talking teddy bears? at-home test kits for sexually transmitted diseases? Play a little. Take every idea to its farthest, most ludicrous, most grandiose extreme. Be so punked-out, post-modern, you make me feel out-of-date.

Most important of all, make me laugh. You needn't tell jokes, although you'd do well to laugh at mine. You are about to enter a silly business. We put rowboats in toilet tanks and make cats do the cha-cha. This isn't brain surgery. It's supposed to be fun. I know you're nervous, and I'll try to make you feel at ease. I'm nervous, too. Believe it or not, it's harder to judge somebody's work than it is to do that work yourself. And while you're sitting there sweating, I'm thinking that someday I may be working for you.

9-3. Jean Lehman. Vice President. Creative Supervisor.

'There's nothing more distracting than a poorly drawn comp.'

The portfolio that catches my eye is one that's extremely neat and well organized. And—from the outside to the inside—visually pleasing.

Of course, the most important aspect of a good portfolio is good ideas. Ideas that are clearly thought out and separate the product from its competitors.

I look for a "big idea" or an idea that's "newsworthy." Past ads for Volkswagen represent some of the best examples of this.

The much acclaimed "lemon" ad for Volkswagen is representative of an idea that's big and newsworthy. The creative team created a startling ad by calling its own client's product a lemon. Then they went on to tell the story of Volkswagen's preoccupation with quality and details, to the point of plucking a few of their own lemons.

Another thing I look for is a polished written headline. I do make allowances for the beginning art director who has not had the advantage of working with a writer. But the more an art director can write good headlines, the more valuable that art director becomes.

Single-page ads represent art-direction skills well. But campaigns should be included to show how to build an idea over an extended period of time.

A wide range of products should be represented to show versatility and conceptual abilities. Anything from packaged goods (cereal, deodorants), to services (banks, airlines), to beauty products (perfume, fashion).

The execution of these ideas is the next item on my list. I look at the choice of typeface and how it reflects the personality of the product being advertised. Whether letters have been drawn or actually typeset, the typography should show an understanding of the craft.

A good, comprehensive layout combines a sophisticated choice of typefaces and art. But those choices won't do you any good if the art is not drawn well. Stick figures don't relay mood, style, or conceptual direction. So it's important to have skills as an illustrator. Learn how to draw an image so that the average layman gets the picture. Learn how to apply color with magic markers to create the illusion of a photograph, and learn how to draw people so they don't look like aliens. There's nothing more distracting than a poorly drawn comp.

I look for an ad that takes all the elements—type, visual, copy, logo—and makes them look like one element. In other words: less is more. This can't be emphasized enough. You should be able to get across any concept with balance, simplicity, and elegance in the design.

If all these points have been covered then you'll end up with a good portfolio and a lot of job offers. The main thing to remember in developing your portfolio, though, is to have fun doing it. The amount of fun you have in creating your ads is directly parallel to how good the ads will be.

9-4. Phil Balshi. Vice President. Associate Creative Director.

'The best portfolios are those that break the most rules.'

It's 11:00 A.M. Your second cup of heavenly coffee is cooling off. Saint Peter calls to tell you a young copywriter is waiting at the front gate with a portfolio, and you've got to look it over, since God's out of town.

You invite the candidate in, adjust your halo, open the book. Turning the pages, you ask yourself: Should this book remain in heaven? Or be sent directly down to hell? Or just dismissed to limbo?

It's always easy to spot a hellbound book. It commits recognizable sins, unnatural acts. Like presenting no new ideas at all, or restaging the best ideas of a decade ago. Or stealing or adapting current ideas of other disciples.

Hellbound books are full of the kind of bad jokes that make you groan instead of grin. Inept analogies that don't work, hackneyed claims that don't motivate me to buy. They bring nothing new to the party. They just tell the same old story but change the names to protect the guilty.

How many car commercials show cars driving straight down a hairpin turn? Why not show that same car making the hairpin turn *in reverse*? How many ads have you seen that fixate on the word "quality"? Why not *show* quality—end-result performance, user satisfaction, peer admiration, or whatever—instead of talking about it? You get the picture.

Less sinful are those books you return to limbo. They're neither good enough for heaven nor bad enough for hell. They contain two ads with great ideas, three ads with good ideas, and seven ads with no ideas at all. There are clear signs of talent, but no sense of *consistency*.

Living in limbo, and working to move up to heaven, is a little painful. Take your best two or three ads, and try like hell to bring the others up to that standard—in visual *and* headline ideas. After enough self-criticism, your work will get better, the gates will open, and the pain will go away.

Finally, there are those few books that make it directly past the pearly gates. They contain very different materials, but all have one common characteristic that separates the saints from the sinners: they don't stick to precedent or follow the rules. The best portfolios are those that break the most rules, that make you think about products and services in fresh new ways you never thought about before. These books are full of ads that make you laugh or shiver. They evoke an emotional, or intellectual, or visceral response that raises your eyebrows and straightens your back. They take the expected to unexpected places.

These heavenly books are full of ads that leave you with a lump in your throat or a thought in your mind every time you turn the page. They are tightly edited—every illustration, headline, sentence is there *for a reason*. And they never substitute an execution for an idea—they make you think about and remember the worth of the product, not the cleverness of the ad.

These books are quick reads, because it's hard to stop going through them. When you do, you say to yourself, "Man, I wish I'd written that."

9-5. Bob Steigleman. Vice President. Executive Art Director.

'Is there a piece in the body of work that is surprising or shocking?'

First, I look to see if the beginning art directors have a sense of the real world of business. They have to be sensitive to the fact that businesspeople are looking for help. They have to understand that if they can help someone do a job or look good they have a good chance of being hired. People in our business don't have the time or patience to teach these basics.

Second, I look for imagination and vision. Do the samples go beyond recent creative trends and, at the same time, does the work suggest that the beginner is truly a student of advertising (as I think all practitioners must be)?

Third, does the applicant have a good sense of craft? Is the work presented in a way that suggests the "author" is truly proud of it? Is it put together with loving care and do I feel that this person enjoyed the total creative process?

Finally, is there a piece in the body of work that is surprising or shocking? Something that stays with me two hours after I close up the portfolio? That's the work of the kind of person I want working for me.

9-6. Ray Dempsey. President, Creative Director.

'Pretty pictures and florid sentences turn me off.'

Ideas are what every creative director looks for when reviewing a book, even a beginner's book.

Pretty pictures and florid sentences turn me off. I'm not out to discover another Rembrandt or Shakespeare. I'm looking for imaginative problem solvers. What interests me is how you think and how relevantly and excitingly you present your thoughts.

When putting together your book, don't bite off more than you can chew. Stick to print. It's easier to express your ideas in that medium. One strong headline accompanied by a compelling appropriate visual says it all. Don't try television. Nobody expects you to do it and most beginners can't do it well anyway.

Always keep in mind that creative directors are looking to improve the breed, not just reproduce it. So if you're going to imitate anybody's style, imitate the best.

Be simple. Be relevant. Be imaginative. Be yourself. And for heaven's sake, be patient. If you have the talent, you'll be discovered.

9-7. John Triolo. Senior Vice President. Associate Creative Director.

'Your book had better look clean, neat, well designed, innovative, surprising, and incredibly well thought out.'

If I were thinking about hiring you as my assistant art director, the main thing on my mind would be that you are going to be doing *my* mechanicals and *my* comps. So your book should look exquisite. The comps should be neatly trimmed. They should be square. There shouldn't be any rubber cement or any smudges visible. I want to know that you have a "good pair of hands."

I pay close attention to the way the type is handled. First of all, do you have any flair at all for type? Do the letter spacing, word spacing, and line spacing look like they were done in this century? If it's press type, is it put down well? If it's done with magic marker, is it done with a confident hand? And is it always the same style or can you handle a lot of different typefaces?

Then I look at the layouts. If every ad is a headline at the top, a rectangular halftone, body copy, and a logo, there's a problem. I like to see a variety of design styles. Type dropping out of halftones. Silhouettes. Diagonal headlines. Something unusual, please.

If you're wondering why I haven't mentioned the all-important concepts yet, there's a reason. When you're hired as an assistant art director, you're hired to assist. Not to do ads. It's very important that your portfolio says that you'd be a good assistant.

Now, we all know that every assistant art director is going to be an art director one day. So, of course, I look at the concepts. They should be nothing less than great! After all, there was no client telling the art director of these ads to make the package bigger or to use a certain typeface. The easiest ads you'll ever do in your life are the ones you do for your first book. You picked the clients. You picked the strategies. If these concepts aren't fantastic, there's no excuse.

It would be nice if you had some things in the book that are real knockouts. Like unusual ways of selling the same old things. Or a surprising way of talking about something that makes people think about it in a whole new way. It's always impressive when a visual idea in a layout helps the concept. When the layout itself strengthens the concept. I don't see this kind of thing too often, but when I do, I notice it.

Remember that before an agency is going to hire one assistant art director, they'll look at fifty books. Yours is going to have to stand out in that crowd. Your book had better look clean, neat, well designed, innovative, surprising, and incredibly well thought out. That's all there is to it.

9-8. Ira Chynsky. Senior Vice President. Creative Department Recruiter.

'I like to see copywriters think visually and art directors write good headlines.'

I'm often surprised by the number of people trying to get into a Creative Department without a good understanding of what is really needed to put together a great portfolio.

The first thing I look for is concepts—your ability to generate advertising ideas that are original, imaginative, and relevant. Because this is your beginner's book, your work should be unencumbered, unrestricted by rules and convention. I'm looking for ideas that are adventurous and surprising.

Your portfolio should be a reflection of your own thinking. It should contain work that is personal, that is not imitative. I don't look for formulas. Dig deep. Go beyond superficial solutions. Avoid work that is clever for cleverness's sake.

Present an old product in an exciting new way. Develop new product ideas. Show diversity by doing both packaged goods and service advertising. Demonstrate that you can think in campaigns.

I like to see copywriters think visually and art directors write good headlines.

For a copywriter, the headlines should be intriguing and draw the reader into the ad. Does the body copy develop and then support the headline? Is the ad informative? And while style is developed over years, is there a sense of style in the body copy?

For art directors, I look for clean, simple, uncluttered layouts and a fine sense of design. Does the visual work with the headline? Can it convey the idea without any copy? I look for basic elements of craft and practical skills. Is there an interesting use of type? Does the candidate have illustration skills? I look for a meticulous presentation of the work. Don't bring me a sloppy portfolio.

I am looking for people who have already made a commitment and investment of talent, energy, and hard work who can step right in and contribute immediately. These are the people I refer to our creative directors, and these are the people we consider hiring.

10

A WORD ABOUT YOUR RÉSUMÉ

People don't get hired into a Creative Department in an ad agency because of a résumé. Yet I see a lot of beginning art directors and copywriters spend a lot of time worrying about them and trying to create innovative, eye-catching résumés. In order to get their talents recognized, a lot of people waste time creating unusual things to send through the mail, or to have hand-delivered to Creative Directors. I even heard of one student who sent around life-size cardboard replicas of herself to agencies.

Do yourself a favor. Spend your time trying to create a good ad. It's the good ideas, not tricks or gimmicks, that will always get recognized—and get you hired.

In other fields the résumé is important. It must paint a picture of the job applicant. For you, trying to break into advertising, what will say it all is your portfolio. Put about 15 minutes toward your résumé and then forget it.

The most important piece of information on your résumé is your telephone number. That's the quickest and easiest way for someone to get hold of you if they like your work.

Keep you résumé brief and simple. Include only facts, and as few of them as possible. Don't brag about yourself. Your portfolio should do the talking for you.

Put down:

- Name
- Address
- Telephone number
- Position desired
- Last place attended school
- Work experience, if any. If you haven't worked, don't worry about it, it doesn't matter
- School honors are okay to put down, but not necessary
- Add references if you like. Don't bother with hobbies—who cares?

The résumé doesn't have to be typeset, just neatly typed. And keep a few extra copies in your portfolio for those who want them.

The following sums up everything there is to say about the subject: A great résumé and a lousy portfolio will get you nowhere. On the other hand, a lousy résumé and a terrific portfolio will get you a good job.

11

A WORD ABOUT SHOWING YOUR PORTFOLIO

It happens to all of us. You start showing your portfolio around, and you start getting a little crazy. That's because a lot of people who look at your work will feel compelled to tell you how to improve it.

You'll find, for instance, that someone will think ads A and B are terrific, but they don't like ads C and D, and they'll tell you to take them out. The next person will tell you just the opposite. Another will tell you to do ads on products X and Y. Still another will tell you to do television commercials. Or radio spots. Or even sales promotion pieces. (I once had someone ask to see all the ads that I *didn't* put in my portfolio.) If you listen to everyone, you'll become very discouraged. Even worse, you'll become totally confused.

I remember one woman who was an A student with a terrific portfolio. Every time she showed her work, she of course got some comments on how to make it better. She'd go back and rework her stuff, take some ads out, add some new ones.

A year later, she called me to say she was still out of work and couldn't understand why. Nor could I. I asked to see her portfolio and was shocked to see how it had gone downhill. It was a case of too many cooks. She had taken too much advice.

You'll have to develop the instincts to know if the

person looking at your work knows what he or she is talking about. Don't try to adapt your portfolio to every job situation.

Of course, some criticisms of your work will be valid. None of us is infallible and portfolios can always be improved. So before you start looking for a job, find someone you trust and respect to look at your work and give you an honest opinion. This may be an art director or copywriter friend or an instructor. Take that person's advice and stick with it.

Remember, advertising is a subjective business, full of some very opinionated people with all kinds of tastes and styles. So getting different reactions to your work will be normal. Don't think there's something wrong with you.

In closing, this is a good business for any aspiring writer or art director. It recognizes talent, and rewards it. Handsomely, I might add. It's where you don't get trapped into doing the same things day in and day out. It's where you can use your mind inventively. And it's where you'll meet a lot of interesting people.